7

SEVEN SUMMERS

OF STALKING

A WHITE PAPER ON THE #1 CRIME AGAINST
WOMEN

C.W. PICKETT

Mushin Press

"I am the woman offering two flowers
whose roots are twin.
Justice and Hope. Hope and Justice.
Let us begin."

Alice Walker

CONTENTS

Forethoughts

HAS THIS EVER HAPPENED TO YOU? You have an eerie feeling someone is watching you, and sense eyes are on you. This sensation happens frequently, it makes you uncomfortable and a little bit scared, but when you look around, you cannot see anyone. The uneasy feeling continues, and one day you know for certain - you are being stalked.

Stalking is the #1 crime against women. A woman is seventy to ninety percent more likely to be stalked a man. Stalking is a crime of men against women. People go through their days watching over their shoulder, making sure they know where their stalker is at all times. This is not paranoia, but a way of staying safe.

Millions of Americans experience stalking every day. As I researched the subject and talked to other victims, it became apparent the courts and law enforcement were not doing their job to protect us.

The reason for the name of my book, *Seven Summers of Stalking,* is that my main stalker is a snowbird. He goes south for the winter, and when he comes back for the summer, he and his buddies continue where they left off the year before. Yes, there are more than one. Bullies run in packs, you know.

This is not a memoir, but a white paper punctuated by a few journal entries. They are meant to emphasize the seriousness of the crime and to give examples of how stalking impacts victims. Unlike most stalking scenarios, mine is a concentrated effort by many people. They contrived the perfect crime and thought they would never be caught. But like all good criminals, they made a mistake.

Throughout these pages, I talk about awareness and education. The purpose of this book is to bring awareness of this outrageous crime against so many people; to put forth solutions that will stop this assault of violence on our society; and to offer advice to judges, law enforcement, and victims. We will look at the seriousness of stalking and the consequences it imposes. We will also talk about the types of stalkers and the patterns they display.

Although the focus of this white paper is on physical stalking, there is also a short section on cyberstalking. The rate of cyberstalking is quickly outpacing physical stalking. A serious physical stalker will use the internet to obtain information about his victim. Electronic monitoring is as simple as a click of a button. A cyberstalker can pose as devastating consequences for the victim as if they were physically stalked.

These unwanted contacts, both physical and cyber, play havoc on a person's life, and this may be the pleasure stalkers get out of the act; watching the victim squirm and sweat. In some cases, only one person is affected. Most of the time, though, the entire family feels the blows.

It is difficult for law enforcement and judges to see the victim's point of view. The complaints seem petty and a waste of time. Not another report of "he's laughing at me"!

If you do not understand, you should try it. Walk a mile in my shoes, live in my house for a week. Then you will know how it feels.

One generation raised free of violence is all it will take to change our mindset and restore order to our chaotic society. Law enforcement and policymakers should no longer delay in instituting programs to stop this assault on our mothers, wives, and daughters. Until this happens, the crime that affects so many people will continue to erode our confidence and our society.

7.5 million Americans are stalked every year

1:14 feel a great deal of fear

1:10 say the actions are annoying but not fearful

Stalking in America

Stalking Defined

1. Making unwanted phone calls

2. Sending unsolicited or unwanted letters or e-mails

3. Following or spying on the victim

4. Showing up at places without a legitimate reason

5. Waiting at places for the victim

6. Leaving unwanted items, presents, or flowers

7. Posting information or spreading rumors about the victim on the internet, in a public place, or by word of mouth

Bureau of Justice

Wanted: One brave man or woman to help disperse the mob.

(A Letter to the Editor)

Murder and mayhem is not new in our country. For fifty years after the Civil War, the KKK pulled blacks and non-Christian whites out of their beds and hung them. A lynching was a festive occasion, with lemonade stands and places for everyone to sit. Mark Twain said people supported such brutality because they wanted to belong. If they stayed at home, they would be ostracized from their friends and family, and that was much worse than watching the slaying of innocent people. He felt one man could stop the hangings if he was brave enough to disperse the mob, but he doubted there was one brave man among 300.

Well, now I am looking for one brave man or woman to help stop this lynching in my life. Seven years ago, three families moved into my neighborhood, and life has not been the same since. They put the spotlight on me to set the scene for their land and water grab. Smoke and mirrors. Blame me and people will not see what they are up to. A tried and true trick used by generals, magicians, con artists, and criminals.

You are a victim of their con if you believe their lies.

The truth is I am not breaching the peace or yelling or cursing at my neighbors. The deputies came to my house 80 times in the last 7 years, resulting in 8 tickets. For what? To stroke my stalkers' egos and to carry on their collusion, with the support of the local law and the "justice" system.

I cannot stop what I am not doing, and I cannot stop their accusations. I did nothing wrong, I tell the judge this, but instead of believing me, he sentences me. I am not a criminal. The criminals are those who lie in court and use the system for their gain. The ones who are stalking me.

I am the same person you have always known. I am not a liar and a troublemaker, like they call me. I do not breach the peace. Instead of trying to drive me out, they could just ask if my land was for sale.

What is wrong is they manipulate the system like they do and get away with it. Not just once, but 7 years, 80 calls and 8 tickets worth of manipulation.

Chapter 1

A Troubled Population

There are two races of men in this world, but only two.
The race of the decent man,
and the race of the indecent man.

Victor Frankl

STALKING IS A SERIOUS CRIME. People downplay the consequences and give advice based on what they think they would do: "Ignore them. Don't let them take your power." This sounds like good, practical advice, but the people giving it do not understand the situation. Their tune would change if it were happening to them.

Women fight for equality, but we are still faced with the attitude that women are second-rate. This attitude is present in the workplace where women earn lower wages than men, and with the unpleasant boss or co-worker that saps the enjoyment out of the job. And she faces disbelief and invalidation when she approaches a police officer about her stalker.

There are different names for stalking because of the ways people stalk. Rapists have different patterns than batterers. Stalking-bullies prey in groups. Intimate-partner stalking starts during the relationship.

The distinction between domestic violence and stalking is thin. When does a batterer become a stalker? Can stalking behavior be predicted? Are there clues that tell the woman she is picking an attachment-starved, potentially violent man?

Emotional or physical detachment from a caregiver in childhood causes attachment problems in adult relationships. The problems do not surface until the scenario is repeated. An adult who experiences rejection from a caregiver as a child becomes vigilant for signs of rejection from his lover.

Experienced police detectives will tell you people never change. They catch criminals by watching their behavior. People have patterns that are easy to spot if you pay attention, including the intimate-partner stalker. Is he too possessive, easy to anger, demanding constant attention? Does he bully and manipulate?

Bullying is a behavior, not a category; a general term for someone who likes to use their power to control someone else. Bullying is a form of stalking, but the term is usually reserved for children targeting children. Bullying behavior is learned in the home, practiced on the playground, and carried into the second-generation family. Harassment, bullying, stalking; whatever form the victimization takes, causes grave consequences for the victims.

When you are bullied, no one believes you. The teachers tell the child, "I don't see it." As an adult, the authorities say, "It isn't happening." Your world becomes hostile because no one will speak up and help you out.

When you are bullied, you are ostracized. Whether adult or child, you become a target for the taunts, the lies about your character, the put-downs in front of your friends. All of this seems acceptable to those around you, but inside, your world crumbles a little bit more with each taunt and insult.

The worst kind of bullying gets you in trouble with the law. My stalkers used the law to perpetuate their cause. Second- and third-level bullying comes from the authorities and the people closest to you.

The bullied child gets punished by parents and teachers for not fitting in. The parent does not hear the child's anguish and assumes she can change her behavior and just get along. Let us reinforce that with punishment. The least invasive - grounded to her room; to stricter punishment, such as spankings.

The teacher cannot put two and two together. "I'm being bullied, teacher, and it is coming out in my behavior." Bad behaviors must be punished, right? Do not consider the cause of the behavior, just send the child to detention for acting out.

The child continues to act out, and as she grows older, the bullying intensifies, and her victim behaviors increase.

The cycle continues until the child is completely victimized. We call a girl a "mouse." A boy is a "punk." Neither is true, but after years of being the brunt of other people's meanness, they become exactly what people call them. A mouse and a punk.

Stalking is an adult form of bullying, but the repercussions are the same. The mature adult is expected to handle the microaggressions better than a child, but do they?

To be bullied, harassed, and stalked as an adult is not much different. How do you report "he said, she said?" Her bully makes the woman sound like a whiner. "What's wrong, can't take a little teasing?"

The stalker sees it as "teasing," but from the stalkee's point of view, this is <u>not</u> teasing. The attention is annoying, unnerving, and "invading my space."

The misogynic attitude that pervades the idea that unwanted attention is acceptable, and even laughable in some circles, must be eradicated. Even men who are stalked are chided by law enforcement and their peers. We have brushed this behavior under the carpet too long, and like all unresolved issues, it has reached incredible proportions.

The ripple of violence reaches to the far corners of our society. Families are the center of society, and when this unit is destroyed, society crumbles. As we will see, stalkers come from troubled homes and adverse experiences. Now that we know the ramifications of childhood maltreatment, it is inconceivable not to implement programs focused on resolving childhood trauma.

Economic, social, and legal factors lead to domestic violence disputes. Policymakers must step up to the plate and sponsor programs that will put the family back on solid ground.

Once this happens, the rate of violence will decrease, drug addiction will taper off, people will be less stressed and more productive. Suicides rates will drop, and bullies will no longer exist. To remedy this upheaval of violence our nation is undergoing, the dysfunctional and broken systems must be taken down and replaced with healthy, proactive approaches.

Crafting more laws is not the answer. Sending people to jail is not the answer. We must put our money, time and energy to better use. We must build families, not destroy them.

Chapter 2

Stalking in America

We do not invent our mission; we detect it.
Victor Frankl

VARIOUS SURVEYS HAVE BEEN CONDUCTED to determine the extent of stalking. Even with the differences in how the surveys were taken, all the results are similar. *Stalking in America: Findings from the National Violence Against Women Survey* (1998) is one of these. The report has been updated, stalking numbers have increased, but the basic patterns of stalking and the effects on the victims stays the same. The information in this chapter is taken from this *Survey*, unless noted otherwise.

The initial screening questionnaire asked if anyone had:

1. Followed or spied on them
2. Sent them unwanted letters
3. Made unwanted phone calls
4. Stood outside their home or workplace
5. Vandalized their property
6. Threatened to kill a pet

> **Women are the primary victims**
> **(4:5 victims are women)**
> **Men are the primary perpetrators**
> **Most are between the ages of 18 and 39**
> **1:2 are stalked before age 25**
> Empowering Communities

There is little difference in stalking incidences between white and black women, but Native Americans experience stalking behaviors more than any other ethnic group.

Men who cohabitate with another man are more likely to be stalked by other men; either by homophobes or by a man looking for a relationship. Most victims know their stalker, but about one-quarter of the participants, most of them men, reported they were stalked by a stranger.

Most stalkers will go on to greener pastures after a year or two, but ten percent of the people in the survey reported the stalking continued for five years or more. Often the woman will move, or the stalker finds a new love (or someone else to stalk). Police warning the stalker to quit is more effective than restraining orders.

Restraining orders have long been known to increase the contact, rather than deter it. The survey shows this is true.

> **100 people are stalked.**
> **50 report the stalking.**
> **12 file a protection order.**
> **9 of the orders are violated.**
> **Only 3:100 stalkers are detained by a protection order!**
> Stalking in America

When the police were involved, the participants felt they should have taken the situation seriously and tried harder to protect them.

Those Who Stalk

Most people are stalked by someone they know. Half of those stalked report at least one unwanted contact a week, many report daily contact. Most stalkers have attachment issues and are very angry. They yearn for affection; some want to build a relationship with their victim, others devalue and disparage their victims. Rejection of the stalker increases the humiliation and anger, which increases the contacts and the risk of violence.

Intimate-partner Stalkers

An intimate partner is someone who shares a romantic or emotionally-close relationship with a spouse, a significant other, or a housemate.

When a relationship goes bad it can turn abusive. Someone obsessed with a love relationship has difficulty letting go. Angry partners before the breakup turn into angry and dangerous partners during and after the breakup

Intimate partners who are abusive are referred to as batterers. In his book, *You don't have to take it anymore* (2006), Steven Stosny, PhD., notes that resentment is the leading cause of anger in the 45,000 battering men he has treated during his career. Resentment is the catalyst for domestic violence. He claims battering men have deep attachment issues and take out their frustrations and hurt on their intimate partner. The RECON study (2006) validates this, noting stalkers are very angry and resentful, and have serious life problems and failures, such as an inability to stay employed or keep love relationships.

Is it a wonder, with their anger and violence? But these same men can also be quite charming. A woman falls easily for his "rough-around-the-edges" character. At the beginning of the relationship, these men are often charming and go out of their way to please their new love. As the relationship matures, the man begins to feed his resentment from his unresolved past and takes this out on his family. Once a woman realizes she has made a wrong decision in choosing this man as a mate, she is in a relationship that is difficult to leave. This is when the violence escalates.

Sensing that she is ready to bolt, the man will become more demanding and restrictive. Often the woman is not allowed to leave his sight, and he uses every trick he knows to manipulate her to stay. This manipulation leads to violence.

Batterers

- A complex relationship that starts out with two people needing each other.
- The insecure batterer begins to isolate his partner.
- He brainwashes her to think she is helpless and dependent on him.
- She becomes thankful for his protection, affection, and financial support.
- She is insecure about job skills.
- She fears retaliation to herself and her children if she leaves.
- He threatens suicide.
- Once battering starts there is nothing she can do to stop it.
- Her self-blame is misplaced.

A child complies with the abuser for protection and acceptance.

The most dangerous time for a woman is when the relationship has gone awry and she is looking for a way out. When she does leave, her risk of harm to herself and her children intensifies immensely. Three-quarters of the women said they were physically assaulted during the breakup, and one third were raped. Sexual assault from an intimate partner carries an increased risk during the danger-zone of the relationship. Sex is used to control and terrorize the woman as payback for leaving (Forensics, 2006).

Acquaintance and Stranger Stalkers

Some men stalk their victims because they want to have a love relationship. The man meets a woman, wants to be with her, and she turns him down. The persistent soul that he is, he cannot take no for an answer and pesters the woman with phone calls, love letters, and hanging around. The love-lost stalker carries minor risk for physical harm; this behavior is annoying but not dangerous.

Rapists

Rapists have a sick psychological bent toward women. Stranger rapists plan their attacks and stalk their prey before striking. The woman often does not know he is stalking her, and this is where her danger lies. Most rapes, however, are committed by an acquaintance; a family member, or friend. Rape from an acquaintance carries not only the guilt and shame that goes with being sexually assaulted, but also a deep sense of betrayal.

The Stalking-Bully

When other people are involved with the plot, not only are you dealing with a stalker, but a stalking-bully. Rapists, batterers, and most stalkers work alone. Bullies run in packs. They feed on the power of the group think - all must agree and act like the others in the group.

Their main rule is to stick together. Back each other up. Make the victim look like a fool.

While the first three types hide behind closed doors and lurk in dark alleys, the stalking-bully is in plain sight; he mingles and charms. He is clever in setting the scene. He discredits his victim by telling rumors and lies, spreading the gossip like cancer. Like the batterer, the stalking-bully elicits support from friends and family of the victim, which further alienates her from a support system.

Defacing the victim is vital to the stalking-bully's success. He puts her in a negative spotlight, denies everything she says, and backs up his word with his colluding buddies.

Now you have a perfectly innocent woman in a very serious and dangerous position. When a woman is stalked, people doubt her word, they discount what she says, and she tries everything she can to get her stalker off her back. These attempts to get him to leave her alone only intensifies the stalking.

He places himself nearby so he can watch her, taunt her, and make her life miserable. Stalkers often move into the same neighborhood as their victim, so they can watch them at will. Their pleasure is in the watching and the intimidation.

A rapist and batterer get off on the physical release. A stalker gets off on the watching. The bullying-stalker gets off on getting away with it. He cannot be found guilty, what evidence is there?

People believe him, and do not believe you. Why? Because you are a woman and do not carry as much weight? Your truth is not as strong as his lies?

The worst part of being stalked is that people do not believe you. You are in danger. You are on constant alert. Psychological assaults are more devastating than physical bruises, and there is nothing you can do to ward off the attacks.

A Profile of Stalkers

Men who Stalk

Stalkers are:
- Generally, in their 40's
- Underemployed or unemployed
- Unable to have healthy love relationships
- Predisposed to pursue people who reject them
- From a troubled childhood

Facts about stalkers:
- 1:7 are psychotic at the time of the offense
- 1:4 are either on drugs or alcohol or have suicidal tendencies
- 2:3 pursue their victims at least once a week, some pursue them daily
- 8:10 use more than one way to stalk their victims
- 1:5 use weapons or threaten to use them
- 1:3 have stalked before
- 1:3 have a history of domestic violence and assaulting their partner
- 1:2 commit violence to person or property

Women Who Stalk

- 4:10 stalk a professional or celebrity
- Stalk other women because of perceived mistreatment from victim
- Follows victim
- Phone calls are the common contact
- No sexual assaults on victims

RECON typology of stalking

Women Who Stalk

Women stalkers differ from men in the way they stalk, the choice of the victim, and their motivation. Male stalkers are love-struck and want their relationship back, stalking women of past relationships. Women also want a close relationship, but their targets are frequently their therapist, doctor, teacher or lawyer; interestingly, women stalk celebrities more frequently than men (Purcell & Mullen, 2001). Women stalkers are vindictive about workplace disputes, especially towards other women who they felt displaced them. Women do not sexually molest their victims and rarely have a criminal record. They abuse drugs and alcohol less frequently than men.

One-fifth of women stalkers are delusional, and often diagnosed with borderline personality disorder, which is highlighted with failed relationships. And indeed, like men, women stalkers have problems with relationships, though not necessarily intimately-related. Or they become angry because they feel slighted, or a friendship ended. Most victims are known to their stalkers. Male victims who report being stalked by women are often ridiculed by police and told to "enjoy the flattery."

Women make contact with phone calls, emails, and letters. They also send unwanted gifts, drive by the place of home or work, and follow their victim. They are less violent than men. If violence does erupt, little harm is done. Women stalkers are Caucasian, age 18-58, heterosexual, and single with no children (West & Friedman, 2008).

Battered Women Who Stalk

These women have a different profile. They are unemployed, in their 30's, and with children. Their self-esteem is below ground level and they are fully dependent on their man. He leaves her broken and twisted with children to feed, and out of desperation, she stalks him. Her tactics consist of begging him not to leave, gaining information about him from others, sending him gifts, showing up uninvited, following him. At its worse, the woman will threaten suicide (West & Friedman, 2008).

Women who are abused are likely to show the same behaviors they experience as a victim.

A woman in an abusive relationship carries the risk of being killed fifty times more than the general population
Stalking Fact Sheet

Cyberstalking

Cyberstalking is quickly outpacing physical stalking, and for that reason it is included in this report. As with physical stalking, cyberstalking causes fear, distress. and anger. Most targets are young women between ages 18 and 24. Social media, gaming communication, website comment sections, and emails are the most common ways stalkers contact their victim. Online sexual harassment and physical threats are experienced by over one-third of the victims (Online, 2017).

Once a stalker has your personal information, he can access anything of yours he needs; bank accounts, employment history, medical history, divorce records, even legal records. The problem with today's information overload is that secrets can easily be unburied; the past is never forgotten. Once something is on the internet, both public information and private correspondence, it stays there forever.

The motivation for a stalker is the same whether on-line or a physical presence. A romantic partner wants to reconnect; a rejected lover wants redemption; a delusional attachment thinks you love him. Revenge and hate are also strong motivators for stalking. You can also become a target just by being in the wrong place at the wrong time; random stalkers mark anyone who shows up on their screen (MacKenzie et al, 2011).

A stalker has one of two goals: Either to take your money or to invade your life. The one who wants your money stays invisible and tries not to be detected. The stalker who wants to invade your life sits on the periphery. He is lurking in the shadows, whether cyber or real, and he wants you to know he is there. Eventually, you will figure out who he is because he drops hints and makes his presence felt. They stay in the fringes of your life; like posing as the mailman, or the plumber. This is why the internet is such a boon for a physical stalker, and so dangerous for you. Anyone can find everything about you with a simple search, and then use that information to find you and stalk you in person.

The psychological effects of cyberstalking are much the same as physical stalking. The audience is larger, the access is easier, and more people are subject to the stalker's posts.

Cyber-victims can be young, old, rich, poor, desperate; the same people who have been taken advantage of since the beginning of time. Modern technology just makes it easier to prey on the unfortunate.

The same rule applies on-line as in real life:
Is this a person you want to spend your time with?
Are they a positive influence?

Social Media

This connector of people has replaced the traditional communication of phone calls and letters. Social media is great for reacquainting with long-lost friends and family, and to get a glimpse into people's lives that we normally would not see. Social media gives us an opportunity to connect.

It is too bad this great form of communication has great risks associated with it. Social media is where the stalkers hang out because there is so much information about you. Your posts cannot be deleted. Once you talk about your personal life, no matter how safe you think you are, anyone can access your conversation.

If you have not done so, try it. Search a friend's name on Facebook and see what you come up with.

The less time you spend on social media and in chat rooms, the less your risk for exposure to a stalker. Limit your time on social media, limit your contacts to only those you trust, keep your posts brief. Share other people's posts, and if you have something personal to say, write your friend a letter, or call them on the telephone.

__Any__ information you post on the internet is potentially susceptible to hackers and stalkers!

If You Fear You are Being Cyberstalked

1. Tell the person <u>one time</u> to never contact you
2. Do not respond to them again
3. Exit the suspicious site immediately
4. Report the activity to the site administrator
5. Save all communication
6. Decrease or discontinue your internet presence
7. Unsubscribe from all suspicious emails
8. Delete your personal information from all accounts
9. Change usernames and passwords

Personal Safety

Like anything else in life, if you do not take risks, you miss out. Not many of us want to live in a bubble. "But I love Facebook!" you say. Love Facebook, just be careful what you post.

People used to keep their diaries locked up tight and hide them under the mattress. Today it seems people have few qualms about baring their souls in public. Because that is what you do every time you tell your friend on social media what is wrong with your life. Even if you keep your business to yourself and use safety precautions, it is impossible to keep your affairs completely quiet in this age of information overload. Privacy is a thing of the past, even if you unplug from both the internet and society. Few people are willing do to this, so it is important to use precautions to stay safe.

We all know this. We are schooled in internet safety, told to change passwords frequently, and encouraged not to post more personal information than necessary. Even so, forty-percent of internet users still experience some form of stalking (Online, 2017). If this group of people would be more careful in what information they gave out, the incidence of cyberstalking would decrease dramatically.

Protecting Personal Information

- Secure the information your children post on-line
- Monitor the sites your children visit
- Stress the importance of telling you about uncomfortable contacts
- Audit your on-line information on a regular basis
- Ask others not to give anything out about you
- When asked, give only the bare essentials
- Have a "web" user name, other than your own
- Avoid on-line polls and surveys
- Password protect cellphones, land lines, emails, bank accounts, credit cards
- Replying to a request verifies your email

Safe with Social Media

- Do not accept friend requests from strangers
- Check out all friend requests before you accept them
- Do not post photos of your home or your neighborhood
- Do not post photos of your children
- Either leave the photo space blank, or use an image other than your face
- Do not post your travel plans or adventures
- Carefully check out on-line groups before you join

Chapter 3

Save The Children

Abnormal behavior in an abnormal situation is normal.

Victor Frankl

APPROXIMATELY ONE-QUARTER, or twenty-five percent of Americans, are witnessing violence at any time. To add to the confusion, eight million children are in the adoptive/foster care system each year. Untold millions of grandparents are raising their grandchildren.

By the time you factor in the people who are wrongly convicted, and the people who witness violent crimes, 1:-2 Americans are involved in some kind of violence.

Less than half of us are operating on all four cylinders. Less than half of the people in the United States wake up each morning happy, eager to meet their day, while the rest of us arise from a cement-heavy bed to put on the cement-heavy boots that we wear all day. Sluggish, tired, little energy or motivation.

How rare to find someone that does not have a problem with a relationship, or the law, or is happy with the job! Here we address one of the reasons for this heavy feeling; being stalked makes a person feel this way.

Effects of Stalking on Victims

The impact of stalking is immense:

4:10 fear not knowing when their stalker will attack next
3:10 fear the stalking will never quit
1:8 take time from work
1:7 move away from their stalker

Socioeconomic consequences:

- financial difficulties
- forced to quit jobs or school
- forced to change name
- forced underground
- avoids social contacts

Psychological consequences:

- takes extra security precautions
- heightened anxiety
- chronic sleep disturbance, insomnia, restless sleep
- excessively tired or weak
- poor appetite
- frequent headaches
- persistent nausea
- distrustful and suspicious
- fearful
- angry
- paranoid
- depressed
- sad
- change in personality
- hypervigilant
- introverted
- more aggressive (10% report this)

The Impact on the Family

When a child dies before the parents die, the parents suffer greatly. The second greatest suffering is watching your daughter live in an abusive relationship and that is all you can do - watch. Whatever you do makes the situation worse, and one day you realize everyone is better off if you step away as far as you can. One hand on the phone, ready to call the police, the other hand pulling in the children to give them comfort - once again. Watching and waiting is agonizing. The mother waits for two things: "Mom, come get me." "Mom, he hurt me." The mother is worried. He is mean and out of control. Her daughter and the children are in danger. She is afraid that final call will not be from her daughter, but from the police, bringing the news her daughter is dead.

One day, hopefully before the "he-hurt-me" call, the daughter will call for help to get out - for the last time. She has made her resolution, she cannot tolerate the abuse any longer. The mother sighs with relief and does everything she can to help her daughter get back on her feet; tenuously waiting for her to change her mind and go back - once again.

This cycle continues until one day the daughter decides it is over. Or is it? She decides to leave, but her man is still hanging around, and the contacts create fear. It is time to end this, but he cannot let go.

After the divorce and the drama are over, the woman wonders what took her so long. Why did she not get out years ago? How could she be so blind to fall for such a man in the first place? She swears she is done with men.

Children are in the middle of this violence, torn between their parents, trying to decide who is right and wrong, lost between two adults who are shattering their lives. If their mother moves away from the stalker, this also has repercussions on them; leaving home, school and friends, and starting a new life elsewhere - often repeatedly moving to avoid the stalker that follows them.

Psychological angst produces stress in a dose-response manner. The higher the dose, the more intense the response. Stalking is a crime that covers years of worry and anxiety. Victims of stalkers have elevated levels of mental distress. Three-quarters of the women who have an intimate relationship with their stalker meet the criteria for PTSD (Blaauw et al, 2002).

Socioeconomic factors contribute to family violence. Poverty fosters incarceration. Or is poverty a result of incarceration? This is a chicken-and-egg conundrum. Children do not learn strong social skills in an impoverished environment, whether economically or emotionally, and lack of social skills can lead to incarceration.

The Role of Loneliness

We learn how to act sociable in the family setting. In a functional family, family members freely express their ideas and feelings without fear of recrimination; and feel safe in this knowledge. A healthy family supports one another in good times, and troubled times, with warmth and understanding. Family members are satisfied and content, and compromise is easy.

A dysfunctional family environment is the opposite. There is coldness, fear of expressing one's emotion, and children feel misunderstood by their parents. This distancing may not be a sign of poor parenting skills, but a of lack of social learning on the part of the parent.

If individual family members can heal, the family heals. With healthy families comes a healthy society. A society where people are happy and productive, not depressed and violent.

People with poor social skills have difficulty achieving their goals and connecting with others. Loneliness results in limited opportunities to practice social skills. With less practice at social interaction, people are more vulnerable to being bullied or becoming a bully.

The effects of bullying can persist through teen years and into early adulthood in the form of poor social skills and loneliness. College students who were bullied as children claim loneliness. This is also the time people are having children, so unknowingly, parents are passing their negative coping skills and loneliness on to their children.

Lonely parents lack the ability to fully attend to their child's needs, are lax in their discipline, and do not engage in socialization activities with their children.

A negative or harmful social situation will affect a person's ability to relate to others and experience closeness. When someone is lonely, they feel alienated, disconnected and misunderstood. Children do not have the maturity to deal with the shame and intimidation they experience from a bully. A child with social anxiety is bullied two to four times more than a socially-comfortable child (Segrin et al, 2012).

A poor environment in the family of origin is a strong sign for troubled teens. When teens grow up in an emotionally-absent family, they report more conflict within themselves and a loss of family cohesion.

Most youth are incarcerated for technical violations of probation, not new offenses.

The Probability for Adolescent Boys Committing Murder

<u>Doubles</u> with a history of:

- violence in the family
- abuse
- gang membership
- abuse of illegal drugs

<u>Rises to three times as likely</u> by adding in a history of:

- a prior arrest
- possession and use of a weapon
- neurological problems affecting cognition
- school difficulties including truancy

Broderick & Bleweitt

34,000 Youth Are Behind Bars

Technical violations		6,600
Drugs		1,900
Trafficking	300	
Possession	1,600	
Crimes against person		13,600
Crimes against property		8,100
Public order		2,200

. A technical violation is a status offense of behavior committed by a youth that is not a violation for adults.

Running away
Truancy
Incorrigibility

1 in 100: America Behind Bars

Chapter 4

Invisible Disabilities

For the meaning of life differs from man to man, from day
to day, and from hour to hour. What matters, therefore, is
not the meaning of life in general, but rather the specific
meaning of a person's life at a given moment.

Victor Frankl

IF I AM IN A WHEELCHAIR, will you kick the chair? Try to overturn it with me in it? Will you laugh at me because I have no legs, and poke fun at me because I am shy? No, you will not. Unless you are malicious and unusually cruel.

We can see if someone has legs or not, and we make exceptions in our minds for that person. People in wheelchairs prove they are not limited, some even forget the chair and walk on their hands. People with physical disabilities have an amazing reserve of patience and fortitude. What "normal" person would spend hours getting dressed in the morning when it would be so much easier to spend the day in bed? Not only do people with disabilities arise and face their day, they do amazing things able-bodied people would not consider.

We hear of people in wheelchairs winning marathons; gymnasts with no legs. Look around. There are people with physical disabilities going about their day just like those with abilities intact. Perhaps you are one of these brave souls.

Do you notice people with nonphysical disabilities? Do you notice the child on the autism spectrum, or the person in torment with spiritual pain? Do you see the veteran going about his day despite the battle with his memories?

I will venture to say you do not. What you see are distressed people in various stages of disarray. But unlike the man in the wheelchair, you cannot pinpoint their affliction. You have no idea what is going on in their minds. Because you cannot identify with them, they become less-than.

We cannot see their affliction so that justifies kicking them when they are down. Anyone that cannot connect, or acts "weird" or seems off; that person becomes a victim to our less-than attitudes.

If a person is in mental distress and out of control, we punish them. The courts are full of people accused for their inappropriate behavior. The schools are full of children in detention because they acted out.

Rather than the courts offering help to people in crisis in the form of counseling or rehabilitation, they throw them in jail - or turn them loose without an offer of help. When an offender is sentenced to rehabilitation or counseling, often the services are not effective, and after thirty days of treatment, he goes back to his old living situation. Where is the help in that?

Rather than offering counseling and problem resolution to the bully and his victim, or teaching self-restraint after the meltdown, schools insist on punishing the child with detention and other consequences.

The behaviors do not change, and the judges and principals cannot figure out why.

This is why. People are kicked when they are down - by the very people who are helping them. The same people who would never kick someone in a wheelchair will make life miserable for someone with a mental disability.

A mental or neurological affliction is invisible. People cannot see scars or disfigurements and consider people with errant behavior are intentionally showing a lack of self-control. We lock them up, detain them, or reject them - kicking them when they are down.

The state of the mentally ill today is the same as it was 200 years ago. The facilities are full. Without enough beds to go around, the outflow goes to the jails. People who are already downtrodden and have problems coping are pushed down even further by policemen and judges.

It is not the fault of the mentally ill to be this way. We lack compassion for people in trouble. We are a society that punishes, not forgives.

Why is this discussion on mental illness important in a report on stalking? We have made the connection between mental health issues and childhood maltreatment, abandonment, and loneliness. Now we must make the connection between these early childhood experiences to the impact it has on family dynamics. Sound mental health is contingent on a healthy environment. When a child grows up in an unhealthy situation, they will struggle with mental disorders and relationship problems in their adult years.

We blame families because they cause domestic violence. We let this escalate until it gets out of control and then we punish the husband for assaulting his family. The courts and policymakers see incarceration as the answer, but in fact, present policies are creating mass chaos for families who are in trouble. Unfortunately, the plight of incarceration affects all families with a member in prison or jail. This is why the question, "have you ever had a family member in jail or prison," is on the adverse childhood experiences (ACES) questionnaire.

The ramifications of incarceration on a family is huge. When the breadwinner goes to jail, the family is left scrounging for food, overdue bills, and face possible eviction or foreclosure of their home. If there were problems before, there are serious problems now. The family is already struggling as indicated by the out-of-control fighting. Now the struggle increases as the justice system steps in and attempts to do everyone a favor by putting the wage-earner in jail.

From our discussion on the stalking mentality and the overview of a troubled family life, we can see most people are not of the criminal mindset. Most stalkers are reacting out of a painful psychological need that comes out in viciousness and revenge. They need counseling, not incarceration.

Lies

(Journal Entry)

It is amazing how someone can put a story together, get a few people to buy into it, and make it believable enough that it sticks. This is what my neighbors did.

There were enough people in on the deal to make it believable. It started with the sex offender. The officer would not remove him from my 7-year-old granddaughter's presence; the neighbors had it all set up, civil standby, cameras. About 10 of them gathered on the road to watch.

The deputy followed me into my house uninvited and continued his barrage. He would not leave, and he would not make the people leave.

It took them ten days to issue me three tickets. The incident happened on a Sunday. I left for Iowa on a Wednesday, was gone for five days, and within 24 hours after I arrived back home, two officers with three tickets and a child protective services worker showed up at my door.

The complaint was vague, another way for my neighbors to harass me, and was unsubstantiated. That means there was no child abuse - on my part - the subjects of the sex offender hanging around all summer and his friend calling her a psycho-bitch were never addressed.

The judge gave me six months' probation and a no-contact order against ten of my neighbors. It took forever to get a court date and they stretched it out to the last minute; four months after the fact I see the judge, add six months' probation on to that, it was ten months before I was clear of the charge. This was nothing compared to the long waits for justice I was about to face.

The next year they hit me again, had their collusion in perfect order, and it worked like a charm. After four months' sweet freedom I am back on the legal train.

I took the plea for the three tickets and only the breach of peace was charged. The next time, I went to a jury trial.

Thinking the prosecutor was fair, and not knowing how she was, I took the witness stand. She fried me. I waltzed into an ambush.

My attorney showed no interest in defending me. He just sat in his chair, but it would not have made any difference what he did - the prosecutor had every means in place to make sure I did not win, down to tainting the jury.

Lies. I cannot believe the lies they told. I was nowhere close to the vicinity where they said I was. Even my half-asleep attorney should have picked up on it.

Lies. I had to slap myself and remind me this was not me when I read the police reports. "Wake up, this is fiction you read." Their statements matched. All lies.

I was their cover-up, so why let anyone think differently? The lead stalker hates it when I go to agencies and complain about him. He calls the deputies to shut me up.

He warned me.

"Shut your goddam complaining or I'm calling the cops."

"Mind your business or I'm calling the Sheriff."

And he did.

Eighty times. He and his wife and friends. All lies. I doubt I will ever live them down.

Integrity, honesty, and loyalty are my three top values. I was taught a person is as good as her word, and I live by that rule.

And now look at me. Called a liar and a troublemaker on a regular basis.

Just so they can steal a road and my water.

It is only a matter of time before the good Lord rains down on their heads, and it will be a mighty show when he does.

"Vengeance is mine," sayeth the Lord. "I will repay."

I just have to outlast them.

Chapter 5

Are There Answers?

So live as if you were living already for the second time,
and as if you had acted the first time as wrongly as you are
about to act now!

Victor Frankl

STALKING HAPPENS IN VARIOUS WAYS and in various places. Work, home, neighborhood, theaters, schools, churches. Human decency has hit its low point in our society. People express their anger in destructive ways. An occasional school shooting has turned into a near-daily event. It seems no gathering is safe anymore.

We must take strong measures to stop this tide of violence in our society. This depends on everyone doing their part.

Trauma is a result of violence. We are a violent society, so people are traumatized. When a marriage is broken, the aftereffects of the breakup touches everyone involved. In the past five years, we have uncovered very valuable information about how trauma adversely affects our mindset and our physical well-being.

We have also discovered that trauma can be resolved. Stopped in the early stages, a child can readjust their brain and move onto a healthy life. The older a person, complete recovery is more difficult, but not impossible. The channels of trauma carve deep caverns in our souls and our minds. The longer that erosion continues, the longer-lasting the damage.

The best way to resolve emotional damage is to prevent it. Unfortunately, many people are caught in the loop of victimization and are beyond the scope of prevention. The answer is to change society's mindset of how we treat trauma and educate families on abuse prevention.

Heart attacks can be prevented. People suffering from a stroke can heal. We take preventive measures during our days; wearing seat belts, as an example. Doctors tell us not to smoke to prevent lung cancer. Why then, can we not take measures to prevent child abuse?

The current systems of schools, mental health, and healthcare are not addressing this problem in a satisfactory way. These are three areas where people are most likely to report their difficulties. The mandatory reporting of abuse keeps people from talking about their situation to counselors, teachers, and doctors because they know involvement with social services is more of a nightmare than a help.

To solve a problem, the first thing is to look at the brutal reality of the situation. The systems meant to help people do more harm than good - or not enough good to make much of a difference.

In this report, we discovered that parents who were bullied when they were children pass on the victim mindset to their children. Parents who were abused by their parents also pass this mindset to their children. This is the cycle of abuse that must be broken.

People with unresolved trauma in their past react to the same triggers in their present lives, even though the original assault happened years ago. This is also a cycle that must be broken.

Aside from eliminating violence in the home, how can we ensure future generations will not experience the violence we have today? What systems can we put in place to help people resolve their history of abuse and prevent children from being exposed to it in the first place?

It will take a combined effort of parents, clinicians, healthcare providers, community leaders, and policymakers. According to Broderick & Blewitt (2010) prevention programs: 1) must be appropriate for the developmental stages of the family, which means implementing programs for all age levels, 2) must be maintained for extended periods, and 3) fail if they are not fully implemented or if they are cut short. Supports must be in place for families as long as they need them. Relapses happen when the supports are withdrawn, so successful programs must be instituted long term.

Wishful Thinking
(Journal Entry)

For the first time in a memory, I am sitting on my deck with all the neighbors gone and relishing the feeling they are gone for good.

I walked outside around my yard, saying to the Heavens, with my arms wide open, "Thank you, Lord, Thank you!"

They are the criminals and they finally got caught. I do not know what happened, but these next few weeks will reveal some interesting events.

It is over. There will be no jury trial. Very convenient, in my favor, this time, to have it put off for a month.

Whatever happens from now on is a formality. How can I explain how I know this? Something in the air? Or something missing? Like the noise and the stares.

The day I envisioned has finally come. Freedom.

***

Oh, my. What a nice dream. But I had to wake up to the reality of more of the same. My jury trial never happened, instead, my attorney pled no-contest with six month's supervised probation. He thought it would help me report any incidences, but he was wrong. Four days after court, my stalker drove by laughing at me, and I took pictures. The next day, they wrote the eighth ticket - another false charge. It took the deputy two weeks and two days to bring it to me after he wrote it.

This will never end.

Chapter 6

Yes, There Are Answers

No man should judge unless he asks himself in absolute
honesty whether in a similar situation he might not have
done the same.

Victor Frankl

THE LAWS OF STALKING. In general, the law defines stalking
as repeated harassing or threatening behavior by an individual;
such as following someone, appearing at their home or place of
business, harassing with phone calls or correspondence, and
vandalizing the victim's property. Some states include laying-
in-wait and surveillance in their stalking laws.

The harassment may or may not have a threat of violence,
depending on the law of the individual state (Tjaden &
Thoennes, 1998). It is difficult to understand stalking as not
lending a margin of "credible threat," but some states make the
element of fear a requirement. The key indicator of stalking is
repeated and unwanted contact, with willful and malicious
intent to stalk.

All states have laws for cyberstalking. For federal cases,
computer crime falls under the Interstate Threats and Extortion
section in the Computer Fraud and Abuse Act. Crossing state
lines with the intent to stalk, to break a protection order, or to
commit domestic violence falls within this act, as does placing

harassing phone calls and emails to someone in another state. The law also requires all telephone carriers provide caller-ID blocking.

As we have discovered, the major categories of mental illness have one thing in common: A history of childhood maltreatment. Batterers, stalkers, and rapists also have a history of childhood maltreatment. What argument is stronger to institute supporting structures, rather than punitive systems, to prevent child abuse and its consequences?

Neither policies nor treatment modalities have made a positive change for most people, and now our society is out-of-control, punctuated with violent acts. Therapy outcomes must be aimed at boosting coping skills, decreasing victim behaviors, and processing the trauma. Policymakers must institute positive, helpful structures for families.

When people cannot control their impulses and lack the self-regulation to live in society, they should be incarcerated, such as sex offenders and violent serial stalkers. A properly-conducted justice system convicts people unable to conform to societal norms. But for the lovelorn man yearning for the attention of a woman that does not want him, prison is not the answer.

Community Sanctions

One in one hundred: Behind bars in America 2008, PEW Report on the States, shows that offenders who re-enter society are more likely to succeed with community release programs than those released without supervision.

Measures that reduce recidivism and prison re-admissions, such as day reporting facilities, electronic monitoring systems, and community service, can regulate stalkers, as well.

Treat stalking and domestic violence as the dangerous situations they are. Combine stalking and domestic violence programs that focus on research and risk management.

Risk Management Solutions

1. The higher the potential for violence and the risk of mental illness, the more aggressive the prosecution and intensive psychiatric treatment should be.
2. Place stalkers that re-offend their restraining orders on strict probational supervision, especially during the couple's separation when the tempers are most heated.
3. Proactive police work identifies domestic violence and the domination before the violence escalates.
4. Counselling and social services offer trauma therapy and family building skills (Mohandie et al, 2006).

Even though current systems fail in meeting the demands of their clients, the inherent structure of social services is not the problem. The problem is the act of putting families through the courts and causing them greater stress than they already have.

Funding and Incentives for Establishing Daycare

A grave problem in rural America for young mothers with infants and preschool children is finding a competent daycare provider. There are not enough daycare centers, and finding a qualified provider in the evening and on the weekends is next to impossible. Daycare centers start taking children at 5 or 6 a.m. and close their doors at 5 or 6 p.m. A single mom who works the evening or night shift is left with friends and family to take babysitting duty. The child's risk of exposure to unlikely influences increases, such as drug and alcohol use by the provider, or abuse because the child is in the way.

The building blocks for relationships and worldview are set during the years between birth and 5. This is a most crucial time for child development. Providing optimal care for the children whose mothers work weekends and evenings, as well as increasing the availability of childcare during the day, will be beneficial all around.

Trauma-Sensitive Schools

We punish children for not getting along with others, when we should be teaching them how to get along. Rather than send the bully to detention, teach him relationship skills, and attend to the child instead of the problem. Teach the bully's victim assertiveness skills.

The schools are the best place to recognize children who are living in trauma and the best place to reach them with counseling. Semester-long self-defense classes teach children awareness of their surroundings and how to resolve conflict. Both martial arts and yoga effectively calm the mind and teach discipline and respect. Incorporating these programs in schools give children equal opportunity to participate and benefit from them, no matter their income level.

With absent father and men figures, boys must be taught how to be men. Gentlemanly traits are never outdated, and by teaching boys to open doors for others, we are teaching them more than politeness.

Mental Health

In the last five years, we have made great strides in understanding trauma and how to treat it. Currently, the most effective treatments are aimed at treating bodily sensations and victim behaviors with neurofeedback (NFB), EMDR, and releasing the experience with sensory-body mindfulness. Talk and exposure therapies do not prove to be effective for people suffering from trauma.

Medications mask the symptoms. Cognitive therapy by itself does little good to try to train the mind to "not to think like that," but works well in combination with NFB and EMDR.

Neurofeedback is helpful in treating addictions and post-traumatic stress.

Since trauma is a physical manifestation, and most addictions are a result of trauma, NFB eliminates the addictive behavior by restoring broken connections in the brain. Children with ADHD and learning disabilities show a remarkable change in behavior after forty sessions (van der Kolk, 2014).

The advantage of some of the simpler NFB programs is it takes very little training to administer. Trauma resolution and counselling is not restricted to therapists and psychologists. By offering a certification training to coaches, physical therapists, teachers, and clergy, resources are made available for anyone who wants to help.

If each school and counseling center had one NFB machine, we could quickly see positive changes in people's mindsets.

Stalking and domestic violence are consequences of an issue in childhood that surfaces in adult relationships. Both women and men are equally affected by their unresolved trauma. When two people who love one another cannot get along, it may well be because their brains are not functioning as they should. Loving connections are difficult when the brain is filled with scattered and compulsive thoughts.

If couples are referred to counseling in the initial stages of their dispute, then there will be no domestic violence call for law enforcement to respond to. Women stay in their situation because they made the decision to love and cherish. It is difficult to leave home and family behind, no matter how abusive the relationship. With proper treatment, people can resolve their issues with their past without upsetting and dividing the entire family.

Legislation can make a difference in citizen's lives by generously funding mental health programs. Policymakers will know their programs are successful when they see a decrease in addictions, suicide rates, and domestic violence. When the brain is functioning as it should, there is no need for hypervigilance and resentment, or to hide behind drugs or alcohol.

Low-income children attending pre-kindergarten schooling have less incidence in juvenile and adult crime, graduate from high school, and have higher employment earnings rates;

16:1 when compared to low-income children without preschool!

1 in 100: Behind bars in America, 2008

Educate Judges and Attorneys

1. Threats and fear are a personal perception. Realize that what may seem benign to an outsider is generating fear in the victim. Consider why the stalking behavior is threatening.

2. Fear is expressed in different ways. Victims do not always show their reactions to the trauma in the way one expects. Consider the fear factor even though it is not explicitly expressed.

3. Does the defendant have past violent behavior toward the victim? Even without a criminal history, the defendant may still be a credible threat.

4. Technology is often used by the defendant to stalk their prey. Ask victims if they believe they are being monitored or tracked with technology.

5. Stalkers often use the children to justify contact.

6. Recognize the effects of trauma and stalking on individuals and families.

7. When a woman says she is in danger, listen to her and do all you can to keep her safe.

Engaging Communities. Empowering Victims

Training for Law Enforcement

1. Listen to your victim. The story may sound unbelievable. Document everything.

2. Build your case with documentation. Show the victim how to build a case by documenting the contacts.

3. There may be other incidences that do not seem related to the stalking, such as vandalism, burglary, and violation of protection orders. Use these incidences to establish a pattern.

4. Become familiar with the evidence required by the prosecuting attorney to build the case.

5. Victims often maintain contact with the offender as a way of staying safe. This must be understood and not judged as wrong. Emphasize to the victim that these contacts increase the stalking. If she wants the stalking to stop she must not give him to reasons to contact her.

6. Utilize listening skills, conflict resolution, and how to stop domestic violence in the early controllable stages. Develop minimally-aggressive ways to deal with the situation.

Engaging Communities. Empowering Victims

Afterthoughts

WITHIN THIS REPORT, we have covered the types of stalkers, the effects on the victims, and how law enforcement, policymakers, and judges can change the prevalence of the crime.

People depend on one another, and when relationships go awry, the difficulties are often overwhelming. Resolution seems impossible because the situation has escalated beyond repair.

We considered how policymakers can rewrite laws to fund programs for families. Families must learn to get along, and it appears the only way they will do this is with intensive training in abuse prevention and conflict management.

Our "independent" society has turned us into narcissists; thinking only of ourselves. People seem to fair better in collective societies, where the family is the cornerstone, and respect is the byword. In other cultures, families take care of family members and do not rely on social services to take the slack. In the American culture, we turn our back on family members and expect them to go it alone.

Putting our child into the world to fend for herself after she graduates from high school may not be the best practice. By doing so, we are sending the message that our young adults are on their own, and they must find their way through their mistakes without our help.

While it is necessary to push our children out of the nest, many of our youth have not acquired the skills to exist in this society. With a high drop-out rate and the dumbing-down of students through the educational system, young adults adopt the attitude that life just happens and takes no planning. They take whatever job they can. People are less likely to pursue a higher education because of the rising costs of college and the economic black hole that comes with student loans.

Lack of education means inadequate housing means low paying jobs means depression and poverty. We are setting our youth up for failure before they even get a chance.

All of this ties into unhappy families. Unhappy families fight.

What is the advice for the woman who is caught in a situation where her mate is ranting and raving and blaming her for their misfortunes?

Stay safe and have an escape plan.

Until the mindset of society changes to where stalking is a serious crime and not just a "dispute," people must do what it takes to stay safe. Staying safe means identifying the danger before it becomes threatening.

Dangerous men are not always easy to recognize. They have all the qualities we love - and then some. But if a woman is alert to the signs that show his dark behaviors, then she can make solid decisions about this person before she falls in love with him.

Love does not happen overnight. Even people who "fall in love at first sight" have reservations. Decide if this person is trouble at the beginning and check him out of your life.

What about the other types of stalkers, the acquaintance and stranger stalkers? At first, you do not know they are there until they slowly intrude into your life. What at first may be annoying can turn in to a frightening stalking situation. Most victims know their attackers. The threat is much less for a stranger stalker attacking than an acquaintance or intimate stalker, so be aware of your surroundings and the people in it, and watch for cues of danger.

The feelings of threat and danger are personal. What seems dangerous to you may not be to anyone else. A man who is threatening to you may seem like a gentleman to another woman.

Do not discount your feelings because someone says you are being too sensitive or vigilant. There is a reason for the fear you feel. Examine the fear.

Advice From Experience

Remember: You are a victim of a crime - a crime that is hard to prove, and no guarantee you will be protected.

You will encounter resistance and denial. If I had a dollar for the times someone told me to "ignore them," I would be rich! How do you ignore a deputy knocking on your door eighty times? You cannot. Nor can you ignore the taunts and the drive-by stares, even though you try not to notice them. You ignore them by not giving them your attention, but inside, you are quaking. How do you ignore that?

It is a safety measure to always know where your stalker is. You learn who he is by being aware of him. You will develop a sixth sense, a proximity sense; you know when he is around you, when he is watching you. You can pick out his voice from across a room full of people.

You must know your enemy, and your stalker is your enemy. You are in a very dangerous situation. Even though people have patterns, they are also unpredictable, and when someone is acting abnormally, you never know what they will do.

It is up to you to gather the documentation. The police want pictures and videos. If he writes emails, save them. Your phone records show the repeated calls. Enlist witnesses and ask them to document the encounters.

Write a letter, then mail it to yourself. Describe the encounter as completely as you can. The letter must be handwritten to prove it is you. If you type it out, notarize your signature before mailing it. These steps are necessary to maintain the authenticity of your encounter. Even if you have witnesses, writing a letter captures the moment in your own hand. Do not open the letter(s) until the time is right. A stack of letters has a powerful effect in driving your point home.

Start a phone log. Report every encounter to the police. You feel stupid. "He's following me again." Even so, report and document it.

The more documentation you gather along the way, the easier it is to prove your case. Stalking is a pattern. The longer they stalk you, the easier it is to show the pattern. Do not brush any encounters aside, document them all.

The proof is on you. Your claim is that you are being stalked and you must prove it. If you have a police officer who is standing with you, you are lucky, and he will lead you through the steps.

The saddest part is that you will lose friends and family, depending the extent of the stalking. After a while, people get tired of hearing about these difficulties you cannot seem to resolve. Having not lived the life of a stalkee, they have no idea what is going on in your life. This is the time you will find who your supporters are, and who will stay with you.

At times, you are so overwhelmed, you will want to curl up into a ball. These are natural feelings; there is nothing wrong with you.

As much as you feel the desire, do not give in. You must live your life as normally as possible. It is important not to give your stalker a psychological edge. This is a game of minds, a game of wits, and you must keep your wits about you. Like any other predator, a stalker senses your weaknesses. Do not to give him the satisfaction of confirming how vulnerable you are feeling.

Every stalking situation is unique, and that is perhaps why this crime is so difficult to prove. If someone is murdered, there is a dead body. Robbery - your jewels and money have disappeared. Before DNA testing, rape was also one of those "he said - she said" situations. The attitude toward rape then is the same as it is toward stalking today.

We have changed our position on other crimes against women, now we must change our approach about stalking. Until the consciousness of our society changes, bullying and stalking will continue to be a grave problem, indeed.

In the meantime, stay safe.

"If You Are Being Stalked..."

Lyn Bates

1. Never interact with your stalker.

2. Do not try to reason with him.

3. Keep detailed records of contacts.

4. Report threats to the police.

5. Get an unlisted phone number.

6. Carry your cell phone with you wherever you go.

7. Keep your gas tank full.

8. Enlist the help of others.

9. Have a contingency plan.

10. Make copies of all important documents.

11. If possible, hide cash for your escape.

12. Check your doors and windows for good locks.

13. Vary your travel time and take different routes.

14. Be careful of posting on social media.

15. Learn your legal rights.

16. If you own a gun, take a gun safety course

Imprisoning the Mentally Ill

It is not the past which holds us back, it is the future;
and how we undermine it, today.

Victor Frankl

IN THE 1970'S, THERE WAS A WIDESPREAD RELEASE of people from mental health facilities across the nation. These facilities were overcrowded, and the people were uncared for. In Wyoming, the State Training School had over 700 residents in a facility that held 100. People were sharing beds and sleeping on the floor. When children with developmental disabilities were admitted to the facility, the parents were told to drop their children off and pretend they were dead (personal interview).

The Weston Act was initiated by a woman who was horrified that her child was treated in such a manner, and as a result, these facilities were emptied out. Shortly after the Weston Act, the mental hospitals also eliminated their overcrowded beds, and suddenly thousands of mentally ill and developmentally delayed people were out on the streets, expected to fend for themselves.

What happened to them? The families who left their children for "dead" were faced with a resurrection of their loved one - needing to come home and be cared for. Families were not equipped for this. And neither were the states. As an answer to this dilemma, states created waiver services and community entry residence facilities. There were not enough services to go around, and people found themselves homeless after having been institutionalized their entire life.

The release of these individuals into society is regarded as the greatest social disaster of the 20th century. The result? America's jails and prisons have become our new mental hospitals (Torry et al). There are three times as many people with serious mental illness (SMI) in jails and prisons than in mental hospitals.

No psychiatric facility holds more people than any jail in America

Office of Research and Public Affairs

Schizophrenia, schizoaffective disorder, bipolar disorder, major depression, and borderline personality disorder are the mental illnesses most frequently found in jails and prisons. For the uninitiated into the babble of psychiatry, below is a description of each of these diagnosis as taken from the mental health manual, the *Diagnostic and Statistical Manual - V* (DSM-5). In brief:

Schizophrenia

Hallucinations, delusions, disorganized speech, disorganized or catatonic behavior, diminished emotional expression. The symptoms manifest themselves between late teens and early 30's. Males are more affected than females. If medication is taken faithfully people can live a normal life, but most people affected with schizophrenia require supportive living arrangements and often have episodes of exacerbations and remissions.

Schizoaffective Disorder

Major depression or mania with delusions and hallucinations. Schizoaffective disorder is on the spectrum of schizophrenia with prolonged periods of depression as opposed to the brief periods of mood symptoms present in schizophrenia.

Bipolar Disorder

There are two types of bipolar disorder: I and II. Bipolar I has both manic and depressive components, Bipolar II lacks the mania. Inflated self-esteem or grandiosity followed by major depression or mania are hallmarks of a person with bipolar disorder. The patient is either up or down, depending on the day. Flights of ideas, racing thoughts, unable to sit still, buying sprees, foolish business deals. Or majorly depressed. There does not seem to be a happy medium.

Major Depression

Many people are aware of the hold depression has on their lives.

Borderline Personality Disorder

Women associate with this disorder more than men. The main characteristics are efforts to avoid real or imagined abandonment. When there is a relationship, it vacillates between ideal and tumultuous. They are quick to anger; for example, when plans are cut short or someone is late for an appointment. Because of their low self-image, they frequently shift their focus of careers and goals, unable to see their plans to completion. They are impulsive; unsafe sex, binge eating and drinking, and spending sprees. There is often suicidal thoughts and self-destructive behaviors such as cutting. The volatile moods that come with panic and anger set the scene for a frantic woman pursuing a lost love. Women with borderline personality disorder were often sexually molested as children.

1840 - 1 psychiatric bed for every 5,000 Americans
1950 - 1 psychiatric bed for every 300 Americans
2005 - 1 psychiatric bed for every 3,000 Americans

More Mentally Ill People are in Jails than in Hospitals

In the 1840's, Dorthea Dix discovered most of the mentally ill were in jails instead of psychiatric beds. She brought reform and advocated for more psychiatric facilities. This system worked well until the 1950's, when the ratio of patient-to-bed started to climb. Today, less than half of the people who need mental health treatment receive it. Not everyone needs a psychiatric bed, most people only need access to counseling.

One bubble off the MMPI* and you are "abnormal." If you look at the answer sheet wrong and get the bubbles mixed up, you can end up diagnosed with schizophrenia or some such disorder. Just by not lining the bubbles up with the questions, and answering "yes" with "no." Or vice versa. Yes, it would be that easy to mess up. Computer programs have alleviated that to a point, fortunately. Here is one place where pencil and paper are less efficient for the scientific method. Too many questions, too much room for error.

*Minnesota Multipersonality Inventory
A test used in assessing competency

At the same time as the Weston Act, when people were dumped out of their overcrowded beds onto the streets, Viet Nam veterans came home from the war. After World War II, the veterans were treated like heroes and were given college educations and money to fund their homes and businesses. This was not the case for the veteran from Viet Nam.

War causes serious problems, and Viet Nam was no exception. Rather than treated as heroes, the soldiers were scorned and called "baby killers." Homeless, ostracized, not debriefed from their experiences, hundreds of thousands of men and women came home from the war troubled and terrified. The diagnosis of posttraumatic stress disorder (PTSD) came from the Viet Nam veterans. Symptoms that were never officially labeled before had a name. Now that they knew what to call their symptoms, they needed help to resolve them. Help is long in coming. Sixty years later, a veteran is committing suicide every hour. How many have ended up in our country's jails and prisons for having a PTSD moment?

By the 1980's, American had a mess of mentally ill people that were homeless and receiving no treatment. When their symptoms appeared, what did we do? Throw them in jail.

States that spend the least amount of money on mental health services spend the most money on their prison systems.

PEW Report to the States

It is illegal to have a mental illness. The Office of Research and Public Affairs (2016) present several problems with treating our mentally ill in this fashion:

Frequent Flyers

People with SMI are in and out of jails so often some call it their home. One study shows that thirty percent are readmitted ten times or more.

The Cost

Prescription drugs cost more than food, especially in our jails and prisons. The mentally ill are frequently required to have a competency exam, which is expensive. And then there are the lawsuits, such as when one family sued the prison after a guard stomped a prisoner to death.

Management

More prisoners with SMI require more staffing. Symptoms increase with isolation. A study of Wisconsin jails showed that three-quarters of the inmates in isolation had SMI, with a staff that had no formal training in handling people with mental disabilities.

Longer Stays

Because of the nature of the SMI, people are noncompliant. They are twice as likely to violate prison rules and then are punished for their infractions. This increases their length of stay.

Suicide

Suicide is the leading cause of death in America's prisons. In Washington state, seventy-seven percent of the SMI inmate population commits suicide, compared to fifteen percent of the general population.

The 1970's was the social disaster of the 20th century.

Releasing vast numbers of prisoners back into society without supports will become the social disaster of the 21st century.

More Mentally Ill People are in Jails than in Hospitals

We are about to experience the same backlash of the 1970s, this time releasing drug offenders and nonviolent re-offenders from our prisons and jails. Approximately one million people. Just like we did then, we release people into society without supports in place to help them.

Average Stay for Inmates with SMI

General prison population

Inmates - 26 days

People with SMI - 51 days

Ricker's Island

Inmates - 42 days

People with SMI - 215 days

Washington State

41% of infractions are committed by 19% of the population.

(Those with SMI)

The Office of Research & Public Affairs

.

BIBLIOGRAPHY

Bates, L. (1999). If you are being stalked... *Women & Guns*. Mar-Apr. http://www.aware.org/women-guns-articles/12-lyn-bates/131-if-you-are-being-stalked

Blaauw, E., Winkel, F.W., Arensman, E., Sheridan, L, Freever, A. (2002). The toll of stalking: The relationship between features of stalking and psychopathology of victims. *Journal of Interpersonal Violence*. 17:50. doi.10.1177/0886260502017001004

Broderick, P.C., Blewitt, P. (2010). The life span. Human development for helping professionals. Pearson. USA.

Diagnostic and Statistical Manal of Mental Disorders. (2013). 5th Ed. American Psychiatric Association. USA.

Engaging Communities. Empowering victims. (2015). National crime victim's rights week. Resource Guide. Statistical Overviews. US Department of Justice.

Forensics Talk. (2006). Profiling rapists. *A Forensic Nurse's Weblog*. http://harfordmedlegal.typepad.com/forensics_talk/2006/09/profiling_rapis.html#more

Mackenzie, R., McEwan, T., James, D., Ogloff, J., Mullen, P. (2011). What is stalking? Stalking risk profile. www.stalkingriskprofile.co/victim-support/cyberstalking

Mohandie, K., Meloy, J.R., McGowan, M.G.., & Williams, J. (2006). The RECON typology of stalking: Reliability and validity based upon a large sample of North American stalkers. *Journal of Forensic Science*. 51:1. doi:10. llll/j.1556-4029.2005.00030. x.

Office of Research and Public Affairs. (2015). Serious mental illness (SMI) prevalence in jails and prisons. *Treatment Advocacy Center*. www.TreatmentAdvocacyCenter.org

One in 100: Behind bars in America: 2008. PEW Center on the States.

Online harassment and stalking. (2017). Privacy Rights Clearinghouse. www.privacyrights.org

Purcell, R., Mullen, P.E. (2001). A study of women who stalk. *American Journal of Psychiatry 2001*: 158:2056-2060.

Segrin, C., Nevarez, N., Arroyo, A., Harwood, J. (2012). Family of origin environment and adolescent bullying predict young adult loneliness. *The Journal f Psychology*. 146(1-2), 119-134

Stalking defined. https://www.bjs.gov/index.cfm?ty=tp&tid=973

Stalking fact sheet. (2014). *The Stalking Resource Center.* Retrieved from https://victimsofcrime.org/docs/default-source/src/stalking-fact-sheet-2015_eng.pdf?sfvrsn=2

Stosney, S. (2006). You don't have to take it anymore. Turn your resentful, angry, or emotionally abusive relationship into a compassionate, loving one. Simon and Shuster. NY.

Tjaden, P. & Thoennes, N. (1998). Stalking in America: Findings from the national violence on against women survey. *National Institute of Justice Centers for Disease Control and Prevention.*

Torry, E.F., Kennard, A.D., Eslinger, D., Lamb, R., Pavie, P. (2010). More mentally ill persons are in jails and prisons than hospitals: A survey of the states. *Treatment Advocacy Center. National Sheriff's Association.*

van der Kolk, B. (2014). *The body keeps the score. Brain, mind, and body in the healing of trauma.* Penguin Books. NY.

West, S.G. & Friedman, S.H. (2008). These boots are made for stalking: Characteristics of female stalkers. *Psychiatry (Edgemont).* 5:(8):37-42. Retrieved from https://www.ncbi.nlm.nih.gov/pubmed/19727274

About the Author

I was lucky to grow up in an era when people were polite to one another and violence was something you heard about in the news. My books are an attempt to encourage people to bring back that goodness, and to stop the craziness that has besieged our world.

My degrees are in social science from the University of Wyoming and healthcare administration from Bellevue University.

Also by the author:

~ *Walking between the raindrops: A treatise on trauma*

~ *Take the quantum leap into abundance: A guide to the good life.*

www.cwpickett.com

Walking Between
The Raindrops

A Treatise on Trauma

~I was the prey,
I couldn't stay away~

C.W. Pickett

Mushin Press

Description

We live in a violent world.

School shootings, mass murders, terrorism, abuse.

Our early perceptions influence our choices as adults. Personal growth is limited to beliefs formed in childhood.

What compels us to do the things we do?

Is it possible to heal from trauma?

Can we break this hold violence has on our lives?

Can the demons of our past be put to rest?

Are you in danger?

Within these pages, you will find insightful answers to questions like these, and more.

READ THIS BOOK TO FIND WHY:

» The past must be processed, not ignored.

» Abuse knows no boundaries.

» Women stay with their abusers.

Together we can make our world a safer place.

www.ingramcontent.com/pod-product-compliance
Lightning Source LLC
Chambersburg PA
CBHW071139280326
41935CB00010B/1294